An extract from the full score of *Bolero* by Maurice Ravel (1875–1937) A *score* is the music which shows the parts for all the performers. This score is used by the conductor.

Woodwind

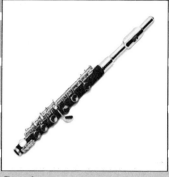

Piccolo

Theme B for Woodwind – Benjamin Britten (1913–76): *The Young Person's Guide to the Orchestra* (also known as *Variations and Fugue on a Theme of Purcell*).

From the pictures above, you can see that each of these instruments produces a sound when the player blows into it. These instruments are either:

1   blown across a hole, similar to blowing across the top of a milk bottle:

Instruments that use this method are the flute family.

2   blown through a cane reed, similar to making a sound when a blade of grass is placed between the thumbs and then blown:

This method is used with the oboe, clarinet, saxophone and bassoon families.

Instruments of the Orchestra

AN INTRODUCTORY GUIDE

Douglas Coombes

BBC PUBLICATIONS

Foreword

The main aim of this book is to introduce in a basic manner, the instruments of the orchestra. The photographs and drawings, clearly show how the instruments are played and how they work. Ranges of melodic instruments are given and in many cases musical examples are provided.

It is hoped that the book will be helpful to people of all ages, who wish to learn and develop their knowledge about instruments.

Many have helped me and I would like to thank in particular the BBC Concert Orchestra, Bill Lewington, Huw Davies and Jean Hoyes (book designers), Alison Bowler who typed the copy assisted by Petra Hirst, and Peter Hutchings who kindly read the first draft and made helpful comments.

Douglas Coombes

Contents

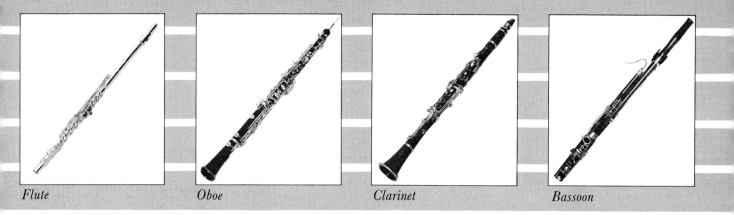

Flute   Oboe   Clarinet   Bassoon

The term **Woodwind** is applied to all these instruments in spite of some being made from metal and other materials such as plastic, ebony, horn and ivory. The name was given to many of these instruments when they were made from wood. As new materials were invented, gradually some were incorporated into instrument-making.

All woodwind instruments have a series of holes bored along the length of tube. A recorder is one of the simplest examples. However, because of the length of orchestral woodwind instruments, many of these holes cannot be reached by the player's fingers, so over a long period an arrangement of keys and levers was introduced. As music became more demanding many of these instruments were developed in this way, see fig. above right.

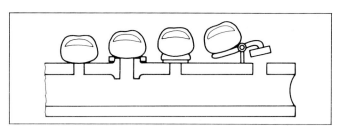

Note the varying widths of the holes. This enables the instrument to be tuned accurately.

A woodwind instrument is basically a tube in which a column of air vibrates – the shorter the tube, the shorter the column of vibrating air, the higher the notes. Conversely, the longer the tube, the longer the column of vibrating air and so the notes are lower.

The Woodwind section in a recording studio

The Flutes

	Piccolo	**Concert Flute(s)**	**Alto Flute**	**Bass Flute**
Italian[1]:	Flauto piccolo	Flauto(i)	Flauto contralto	Flauto basso
French.	Petite Flûte	Grande(s) Flûte(s)	Flûte Alto	Flûte Basse
German:	Kleine Flöte	Grosse Flöte(n)	Altflöte	Bassflöte
Length:	30 cm	66 cm	86 cm	128 cm (total length of tube)

Range[2]:

Footnote

1 Names of the instruments are given in the four main languages found in orchestral scores – English, Italian, French and German.

2 The range of instruments given show the normal working compass. However some virtuoso players can reach higher notes on some instruments and even lower notes (eg low brass pedal notes). In all the examples in this book, the range gives the actual sounds.

Flute

The flute player, or flautist (in USA – flutist) holds the instrument horizontally and to the right. He blows across a hole which is towards the upper end:

The flute does not use a reed. As with all woodwind instruments, different notes are obtained by opening and closing the holes by the use of fingers and keys. The flute is extremely agile throughout its range, and its music often contains fast scales and exciting leaps and skips. The higher notes are brilliant in sound, but the lower notes have a warm, velvet-like quality.

Piccolo

The piccolo is half the size of a flute and has the highest pitch of all orchestral instruments. The sound, especially the higher notes, is very piercing and can be heard even when the full orchestra is playing. However, as with most instruments, the piccolo is capable of delicate and quiet playing. The name is derived from the Italian *flauto piccolo* which means 'little flute'. To avoid using leger lines when playing high notes:

music for the piccolo is written an octave lower than it sounds:

Maurice Ravel (1875–1937): *Daphnis and Chloé*

Alto Flute

This instrument plays a perfect fourth lower than the concert flute and is built in G. Mistakenly often called the Bass Flute in G, the Alto Flute in G is a transposing instrument with music written a fourth higher than its actual sound:

Written:

Actual sounds:

Igor Stravinsky (1882–1971): *The Rite of Spring*

The most effective and individual part of its range lies in the lower octave and a half: which produces a rich, soft sound.

Bass Flute

The tube of this twentieth century invention is so long that it is bent into a U shape so that it can be played like other flutes. Music is written an octave higher than it sounds and written in the treble clef:

Written:

Actual sounds:

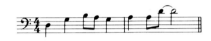

A great amount of breath is needed for this instrument. It is more often used in music for films and in 'pop' music where because of its quiet sound, it is often played close to a microphone.

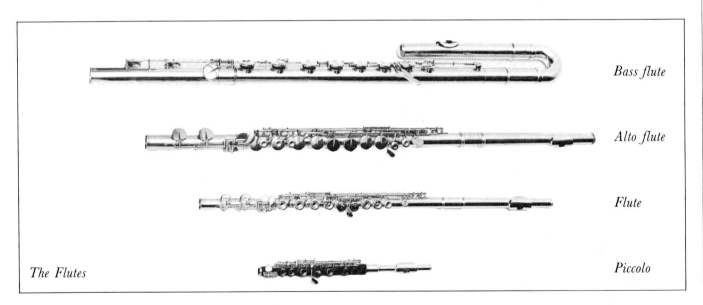

The Flutes

Bass flute

Alto flute

Flute

Piccolo

Compass of Flutes (the dot denotes middle C)

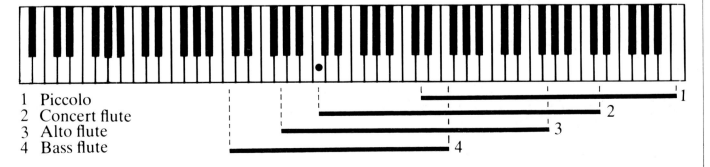

1 Piccolo
2 Concert flute
3 Alto flute
4 Bass flute

The Oboes

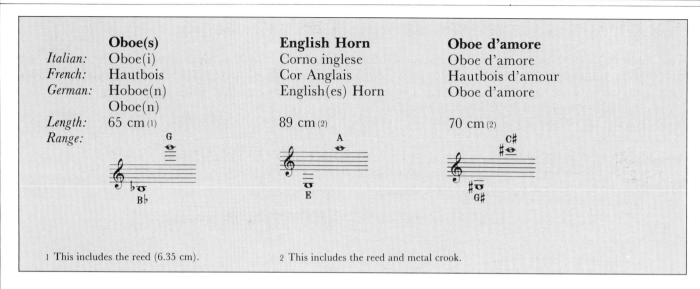

	Oboe(s)	**English Horn**	**Oboe d'amore**
Italian:	Oboe(i)	Corno inglese	Oboe d'amore
French:	Hautbois	Cor Anglais	Hautbois d'amour
German:	Hoboe(n)	English(es) Horn	Oboe d'amore
	Oboe(n)		
Length:	65 cm (1)	89 cm (2)	70 cm (2)
Range:			

1 This includes the reed (6.35 cm). 2 This includes the reed and metal crook.

Oboe

The oboe family is played with a double reed. This is made from two pieces of thin cane, bound together around a small metal tube. A small space is left between these two pieces so that the air passing through causes them to vibrate.

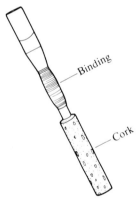

The sound of an oboe is penetrating and has a somewhat nasal and plaintive quality. Rhythmic passages can be played with great neatness:

Gioachino Rossini (1792–1868):
Overture – The Silken Ladder

Melodies of an expressive, almost song-like quality are particularly suited to the instrument:

Robert Schumann (1810–1856): *Symphony No. 2*

Oboe, Cor Anglais and Oboe d'amore

The oboe, with its stable pitch and its distinct 'reedy' sound, gives the A at the start of the concert, so that the other instruments can tune to it.

English Horn or Cor Anglais

Cor anglais means English horn, but it is neither English nor a horn. It is not clear how it came to be called a cor anglais. One theory is that the name is a corruption of cor anglé which means bent horn (if you look carefully at the top of the instrument you will see the bent metal tube). The sound of the instrument is not quite so penetrating as that of the oboe, and though it is equally agile, the English horn is particularly beautiful when playing a sustained, smooth melody:

Hector Berlioz (1803–1869):
Overture: The Roman Carnival

The English horn is pitched a perfect fifth below the oboe. As the fingering of both instruments is basically the same, the fingering for a G on the oboe, would produce a C (a perfect fifth lower) on the English horn. So the notes for an English horn are written a perfect fifth higher than they actually sound. Therefore the start of the Schumann example given above sounds:

Instruments that have their music written down at a different pitch to their actual sounds are called *transposing instruments.*

Oboe d'Amore

This is also a transposing instrument. It is pitched in A, a minor third below the oboe. The notes therefore sound a minor third lower than written:

Written:

Actual sounds:

The fingering of the oboe d'amore and the oboe is identical.

    The oboe d'amore is gentler in tone than that of the oboe and English horn. It was used in the Baroque period, particularly by Johann Sebastian Bach (1685–1750). However it has been used from the beginning of the twentieth century in such works as Claude Debussy's (1862–1918): *Gigues:*

Compass of Oboes

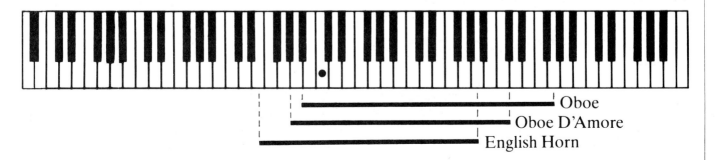

The Clarinets

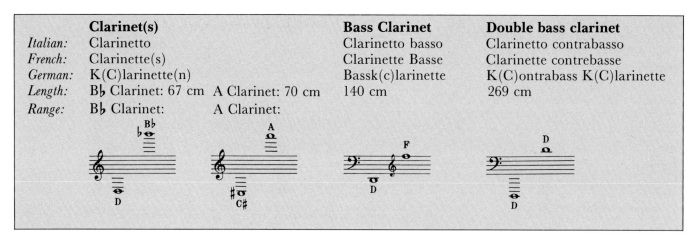

	Clarinet(s)		Bass Clarinet	Double bass clarinet
Italian:	Clarinetto		Clarinetto basso	Clarinetto contrabasso
French:	Clarinette(s)		Clarinette Basse	Clarinette contrebasse
German:	K(C)larinette(n)		Bassk(c)larinette	K(C)ontrabass K(C)larinette
Length:	B♭ Clarinet: 67 cm	A Clarinet: 70 cm	140 cm	269 cm
Range:	B♭ Clarinet:	A Clarinet:		

Clarinet

The clarinet is a single reed instrument. The sound is made by causing the reed to vibrate against the mouthpiece as air is passed through. This in turn makes the air column in the pipe vibrate.

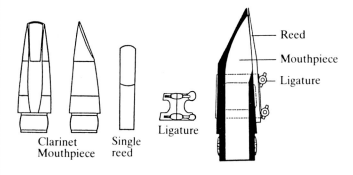

Clarinet Mouthpiece   Single reed   Ligature

Reed
Mouthpiece
Ligature

Claude Debussy (1862–1918): *Première Rhapsodie*

The low part of the instrument (called the chalumeau, after an ancestor of the clarinet) produces a dark, dramatic and rich sound. The middle register is quite bright, while the higher notes are brilliant and penetrating. The clarinet has greater dynamic variation than other woodwind instruments. It can almost rival the flute for agility, rapid scales and arpeggios.

Clarinets have been made in various sizes, but the B♭ and the A are now the two major ones in use today. As all the clarinets have the same fingering, different sizes produce different notes. So for example middle C on a C clarinet sounds as written but on a B♭ clarinet a written middle C sounds:

On an A clarinet, it sounds:

Compass of Clarinets

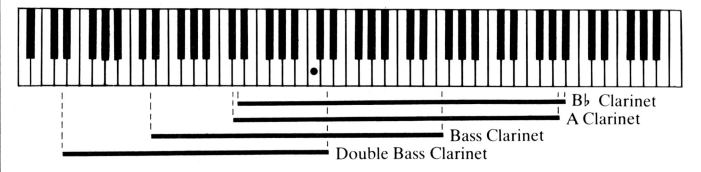

B♭ Clarinet
A Clarinet
Bass Clarinet
Double Bass Clarinet

Therefore music for a B♭ clarinet has to be written a major 2nd higher (a tone) than it sounds and for an A clarinet, it has to be written a minor 3rd higher than it sounds:

The type of clarinet (B♭ or A) is selected by the composer and depends on which clarinet uses the fewest sharps or flats.

Bass Clarinet

At one time the instrument was similar to the clarinet, but it was too awkward to manage. The end of the instrument was near the floor which meant that much of the sound was lost. So these problems came to be solved by bending the top and bottom of the instrument. The bass clarinet is more powerful and less reedy in sound than the ordinary clarinet. The lower notes are very rich and resonant and can be played very quietly. In spite of its size, it can play quick passages with surprising lightness.

Music for the bass clarinet is normally written in the treble clef and sounds a ninth lower than written:

This is known as French notation. However a number of composers have used the German notation with the music written a tone higher than it sounds. So the music above would be written:

Double Bass Clarinet

This instrument, designed in the late 19th century in Germany and France, was really developed by Leblanc of Paris in the 1950s. It has been used by composers such as Antonin Dvorak: *The Devil and Kate* (1899), Arnold Schoenberg: *Five Orchestra Pieces* (1909) and Iannis Xenakis: *Polytope* (1967). Unofficially, it has been added by conductors to double the double basses discreetly.

Double bass Clarinet   *Bass Clarinet*   *B♭ Clarinet*   *A Clarinet*

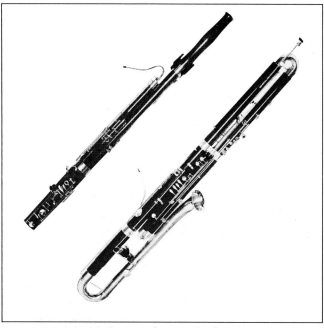

Bassoon and double bassoon (see overleaf)

The Bassoons

	Bassoon(s)	Double Bassoon (Contrabassoon)
Italian:	Fagotto(i)	Contrafagotto
French:	Basson(s)	Contrebasson
German:	Fagott(e)	K(C)ontrafagott
Height:	137 cm	144 cm
Range:		

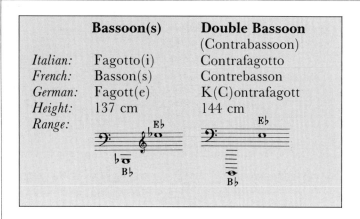

Paul Dukas (1865–1935): *The Sorcerer's Apprentice*

Another quality of the bassoon is its ability to blend with other instruments, particularly other woodwind and horns.

Bassoon *(see illustration on page 11)*

The bassoon has a tube of about 2½ m in length, which is doubled back on itself to make it manageable. It is a double reed instrument (like the oboe) and is the natural bass of the woodwind family. Often called 'the clown of the orchestra' because of the comical effects it can make, it can also produce solemn and gentle sounds:

Modest Musorgsky (1839–1881)
(orchestrated Maurice Ravel):
The Old Castle (Pictures from an Exhibition).

The bassoon is particularly effective at playing short, sharp notes (staccato playing):

Double Bassoon

The double bassoon (or contrabassoon) has a tube just under 5 m long and is folded four times. It plays an octave lower than the ordinary bassoon and is the deepest sounding orchestral instrument. The double bassoon has a dark, growling quality and is generally used to give a strong bass for the woodwind. It is often used to reinforce the double bass part and also to give a strong bass for brass chords. However it can be used for novel solo effects:

Maurice Ravel: *Beauty and the Beast (Mother Goose Suite)*

Music for the double bassoon is written an octave higher than it sounds:

Compass of Bassoons

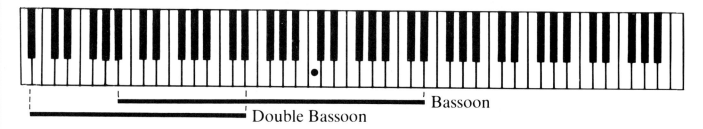

The Saxophones

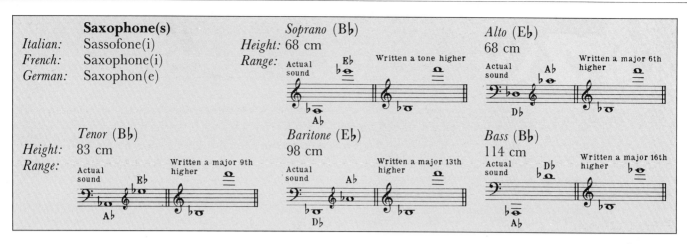

The saxophone was invented in the 1840s by the Belgian instrument maker, inventor and clarinettist, Adolphe Sax (1814–1894). By 1846 there were fourteen different sizes, but the five shown below are the ones mainly in use today. Though made of brass, the instruments come under the woodwind family as they have a single reed (like the clarinets) and use a similar system of keys and levers to cover and uncover the holes. As the fingering is similar to that of a clarinet, players often double on clarinet and saxophone.

Saxophones have a wide dynamic range and can be very agile. Though they have not found a permanent place in the symphony orchestra, the saxophones are used in big band, jazz music, rock and popular music.

The fingering on all the saxophones is the same in relation to the written note. But because the instruments vary in size and key, the actual sound changes. So for example middle C: written for each instrument sounds:

Saxophones have been slow to be used in symphony orchestras but the alto has been used in such works as

Ambroise Thomas: *Hamlet* (1868), Georges Bizet: *L'Arlésienne* (1872), William Walton's *Belshazzar's Feast* (1930–31), Zoltán Kodály: *Háry János* (1926) and Ralph Vaughan Williams: *Job* (1930).

The Sopranino (in f), alto and tenor have been used in Maurice Ravel: *Bolero* (1928) whilst the tenor has been used by Vaughan Williams: *Symphony No. 4* (1935) and Sergey Prokofiev: *Romeo and Juliet* (1935–36).

Saxophones, from left to right: Bass, Baritone, Soprano, Alto and Tenor

Compass of Saxophones

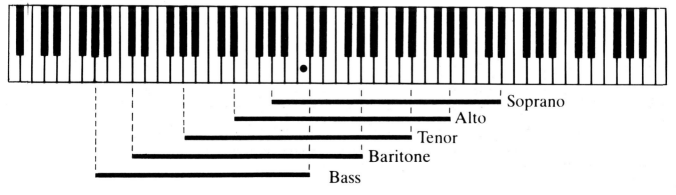

Brass

French Horn

Trumpet

Theme C for Brass – Benjamin Britten: *The Young Person's Guide to the Orchestra.*

A brass instrument has three basic features:
1   A long tube that may be bent into various shapes,
2   A cup-shaped mouthpiece which is inserted into one end of the tube, and
3   At the other end of the tube, a flared bell.

The different 'bells' at the end of the instruments can be seen in the pictures, but the following cross-section drawings of the average mouthpieces for the various instruments will give you an idea of the variety of styles:

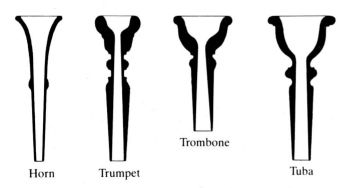

Notes are obtained by means of lip tension while blowing. A tube when blown will produce a series of notes called the *harmonic series*. The lowest note is called the *fundamental*. The pitch of the fundamental is determined by the length of tube. For example, a tube 228·60 cm long should be capable of producing the following harmonic series:

Further notes are available by using valves or slides according to the instrument.

Modern brass instruments have extra piping, and valves are used so that these extra pieces may be added in order to lengthen the main tube. For example, on the trumpet when the piston valve is not pressed down the air goes straight into the main tube, see fig. *a* below:

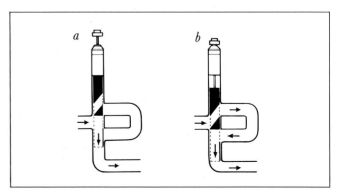

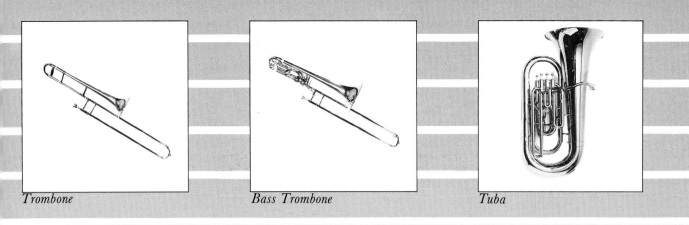

Trombone　　　　*Bass Trombone*　　　　*Tuba*

When a lower note is required the tube is lengthened by the piston valve being pressed down, which allows the air to go into the valve tube before going into the main tube, see fig. *b* (page 14).

The sound of brass instruments can be altered by placing a cone-shaped stopper called a *mute* into the bell. This makes the sound subdued if played quietly, or strident if played loudly.

Brass players of the BBC Symphony Orchestra 1961.

Compass of Brass instruments

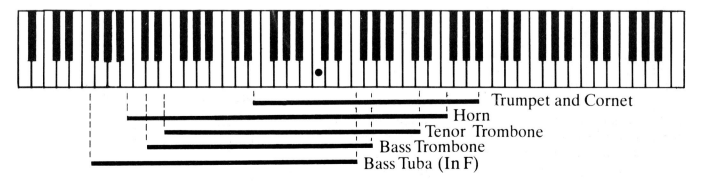

Trumpet and Cornet
Horn
Tenor Trombone
Bass Trombone
Bass Tuba (In F)

French Horn

	Horn(s)
Italian:	Corno(i)
French:	Cor(s)
German:	Horn(Hörner)
Size:	40 cm high
Range:	

Early horns, as the name implies, were made from hollowed-out animal horns. Later these instruments were made from metal, and because of their power they were used outdoors for signals, especially for battle and hunting calls. Hunting horns became circular so that they could easily be carried by the player over the shoulder or over his head and under one arm.

When the horn was first used in the orchestra, it could only play the notes of its harmonic series. If the music changed key, then the player would have, in theory, to change to a suitable horn. It was soon realised that varying the length of the tube would be an asset. So extra tubes called 'crooks' were used:

A crook   *Horn with crooks (late 18th century)*

But no matter how many crooks were used, the player still only had available the harmonic series of the total length. When writing music, composers had to give players time to change crooks.

Some help to players was forthcoming when, in the middle of the 18th century, it was discovered that different notes could be obtained by placing the hand

French horn

Making hunting horns – 18th century engraving

right into the bell. But the sound of these extra notes were different in quality from the main notes. Then in about 1815, the invention of the valve system did away with the crooks. It meant that with extra tubing permanently attached to the horn, the tree valves used in combination could shorten or lengthen the tube, and so produce a wide range of notes.

The modern French horn (tube length including valves about 5 m) is a transposing instrument. It is normally in F so its music is written a perfect fifth higher than the actual sounds:

Pyotr Tchaikovsky (1840–1893): *Symphony No. 5*

Many players now use a double horn. This has a fourth valve which sets the instrument into B flat (a fourth higher than the F horn). This allows greater control of the high notes.

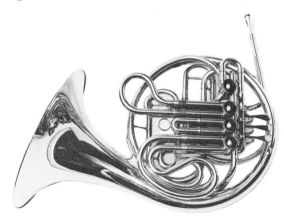

A double horn.

The French horn with its mellow sound can be powerful and majestic or it can produce quiet, mysterious sounds. It blends well with either woodwind or brass.

The French horn can be muted (*con sordino*) which gives the sound a far-away, distant quality. The player has to sometimes play 'stopped' notes. For this, the hand is placed firmly into the bell. When played gently, the sound becomes very quiet, once again distant, but the sound is somewhat thinner. The sign used for stopped notes is +. When the note is to be played normally then ○ (open) is written over the note. Notes without these signs are always played normally.

Another effect is *cuivré* (French for brassy). The player forces the hand into the bell and blows very hard. The resulting sound is truly brassy.

Many solos have been written for the instrument including this one from Dmitry Shostakovich's (1906–1975): *Symphony* No. 5:

The player is asked to play the high B only if it can be played quietly.

NB Though called a French horn, probably because of earlier developments in France, it is usually referred to as the horn.

French Horns in concert.

Trumpet

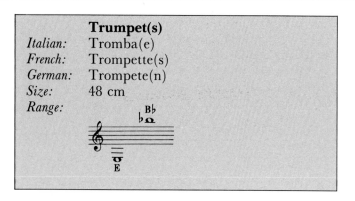

	Trumpet(s)
Italian:	Tromba(e)
French:	Trompette(s)
German:	Trompete(n)
Size:	48 cm
Range:	

A modern trumpet

The trumpet is the most brilliant sounding of all brass instruments and traditionally it has been used for fanfares and flourishes, for ceremony and great occasions. It is one of the oldest brass instruments. Two trumpets were discovered in the tomb of Tutankhamun in 1923 which dates these two instruments to about 1350 BC.

The notes of these trumpets were based on the harmonic series (see page 14). But by the 17th and early 18th century, players specialised in playing the high notes of the harmonic series. As these upper harmonics were close together, it was possible to play tunes. This high register is called the *clarino*. For some unknown reason this technique of high trumpet playing suddenly declined in the middle of the 18th century.

A modern replica, the trumpet in D, has been used since about 1960 to recreate the sounds of the baroque period, see photograph below.

Before the valve was invented (*c*.1815), players used crooks – even a slide trumpet and a keyed trumpet were invented.

But after 1815, by using the valve system, trumpets could be played with great subtlety and agility, with an extended controllable range.

A number of mutes can be used in the trumpet. These include a *straight* mute which creates a soft distant sound when the trumpet is played quietly; but when played forcefully, the trumpet produces a piercing, sinister sound.

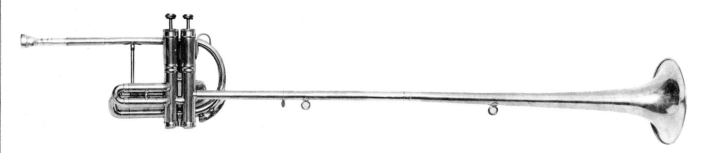

A modern replica of an eighteenth century trumpet

Benjamin Britten – *The Young Person's Guide to the Orchestra.*

Other mutes are the *wow-wow* and *cup* which produce the softest sounds of the three mutes mentioned.

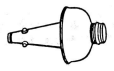

1 Straight   *2 Wow-wow*   *3 Cup*

Trumpets have generally been pitched in B♭, with music written a tone higher than the actual sound (compare with the B♭ clarinet). In recent times, trumpets in C have become quite common. (The C trumpet sounds as written.) The tube length of the B♭ trumpet is approximately 127 cm.

Cornet(s)	
Italian:	Cornetto(i) a pistoni
French:	Cornet(s)-à-pistons
German:	Cornett(e)
Size:	35 cm
Range:	

A young trumpet player

A Cornet

The cornet, which has the same range and tube length as the trumpet, was invented in France about 1825. Its tone is less brilliant than the trumpet but it is just as agile.

Malcolm Arnold (b1921):
Overture: Beckus the Dandipratt

The cornet is a B♭ instrument, so the music is written a tone higher than the actual sounds.

Tenor Trombone

	Tenor Trombone(s)
Italian:	Trombone(i) tenore(i)
French:	Trombone(s)
German:	(Tenor) posaune(n)
Size:	114 cm long
Range:	

Bass Trombone

	Bass Trombone
Italian:	Trombone basso
French:	Trombone Basse
German:	Bassposaune
Size:	116 cm
Range:	

The trombone has changed very little in design during the past 400 years. Instead of valves, the trombone has a movable slide which lengthens or shortens the tube. The fundamentals (pedal notes) of the first three positions can be played if time is allowed within a piece of

Three trombones are usually used in an orchestra and the lowest part is frequently played by the bass trombone. As you can see from its range, it allows extra notes to be played at the bottom of the trombone range. The trombone can be muted similarly to the trumpet.

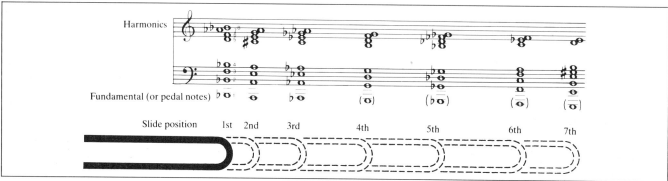

The Harmonic series of the tenor trombone

music to prepare for the note. The tone quality is quite good but this quality gets progressively worse with the fundamentals of positions 4–7.

The trombone is not so brilliant in sound as the trumpet but it has great penetrating power, especially in the high register. At the bottom of the range it can produce not only extremely quiet, soft sounds, but also dramatic, strong sounds with powerful crescendi. Melodies that are solemn and full of dignity are particularly suitable for the trombone. One particular effect is a comic one of allowing all the sounds to be heard while moving the slide. This is called a *glissando*.

Aaron Copland (b1900): *Buckaroo Holiday (Rodeo)*

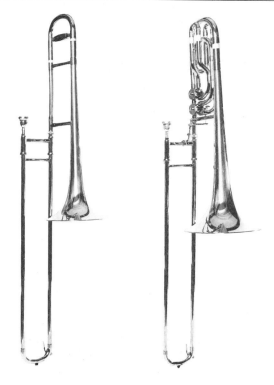

Tenor trombone   Bass trombone

Tuba

(Bass) Tuba	
Italian:	Tuba (bassa)
French:	Tuba (Basse)
German:	(Bass) tuba
Size:	120 cm high
Range:	

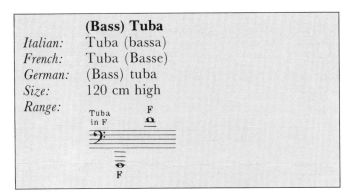

A young admirer of the tuba

A Tuba

soft, smooth playing in the middle register. The low notes can also be played quiet but in the higher register the notes are more difficult to produce quietly. When played loudly, the tuba makes a strong, hearty sound which is capable of being heard when the full orchestra is playing.

Richard Wagner (1813–1883):
Overture – The Mastersingers

Tubas come in various sizes but the bass tuba in F is the most often used in the modern orchestra. The tube length is about 4½m.

The tuba is the lowest sounding brass instrument and is therefore most often used as the bass of the brass family. Because of its size, the bell points up in the air. As it requires a lot of breath to produce the sound, it is used sparingly. As a solo instrument it can produce

Strings

Violin

Viola

Theme D for Strings – Benjamin Britten: *The Young Person's Guide to the Orchestra*

The violin, viola, violoncello (shortened to 'cello) and the double bass form the largest section of the orchestra. They are the backbone of the orchestra and generally they play for most of the time. Basically the sound is produced by playing a taut string (made usually of gut, nylon or wire) with a bow. This bow is made of a springy stick with horse hair stretched along it.

The pitch of any string can be altered by placing a finger of the left hand (string players are normally right handed) on the string and pressing it down on the fingerboard. In this way the length of the vibrating string is shortened and the shorter the string, the higher the sound.

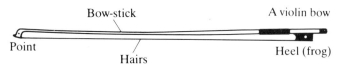

The length of bows is approximately: violin – 72 cm; viola – 75 cm; cello – 72 cm; double bass 70 cm.

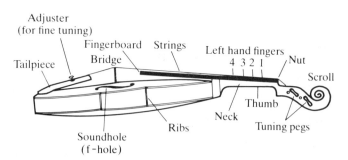

This way of making a sound has led to string players being known as 'the scrapers of horse hair on cat gut'. The gut, by the way, comes from sheep and not cats.

Different notes can also be produced according to the looseness, thickness and length of string. The shorter,

22

Cello   *Double Bass*   *Harp*

thinner and tighter the string, the higher the note. The longer, thicker and looser the string, the lower the note.

Stringed instruments may be played in a variety of ways, and the following glossary will show their versatility:

Col legno (with the wood)   turning the bow over so that the strings are struck with the wood instead of the bow

Con sordino (with the mute)   putting a small damper made of wood, metal, bone or other materials over the bridge. This produces a soft veiled quality of sound

Double stopping   stopping two strings at once so that the two notes can be played together

Glissando   sliding the finger up and/or down a string while bowing it

Harmonics   these are flute-like sounds made by very lightly touching the string at certain points instead of firmly pushing them down on the fingerboard

Pizzicato   the strings plucked with the fingers

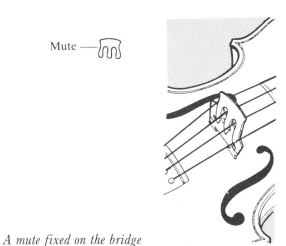

Mute

A mute fixed on the bridge

Quadruple stopping   stopping four strings at once

Stopping   placing a finger (fingers) on a string (strings) to change the pitch of a note (notes)

Sul ponticello (on the bridge)   playing with the bow near the bridge which produces a glassy and metallic sound

Sul tasto (on the fingerboard)   playing with the bow over the upper edge of the fingerboard which produces a very soft sound

Triple stopping   stopping three strings at once.

Compass of strings (ordinary compass and not including harmonics)

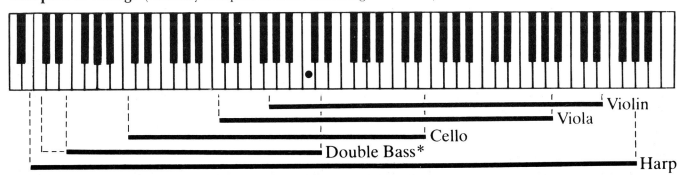

Violin
Viola
Cello
Double Bass*
Harp

* Some Double Basses have a 5th string which is tuned to that very low C.

	Violin(s)
Italian:	Violino(i)
French:	Violon(s)
German:	Violine(n)
Length:	60 cm
Range:	

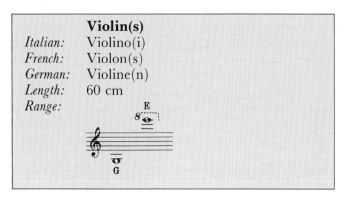

Violin and bow

During the sixteenth century viols were popular and for a time were used with the violins.

The viols, though bearing similarities in shape to the violins, came from a different family of stringed instruments. With their fretted necks and six strings, the viols have more of the characteristics of the renaissance lute. In Spain, in the late 15th century, musicians had used a bow on the guitar-like VIHUELA, normally a plucked instrument. This idea was taken further by Italian musicians and just before 1500 the first true viol came into existence.

The three most important members of the viol family are:

The violin (which means small Viola – Viol-ino), first appeared around the early part of the sixteenth century. No one is quite sure who invented it, but its early ancestors included the medieval fiddle and the rebec.

Medieval fiddle and bow

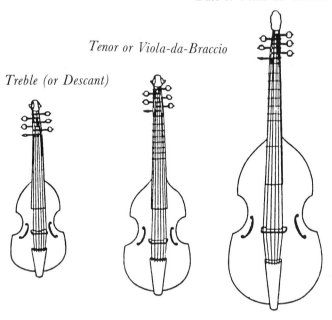

Bass or Viola-da-Gamba

Tenor or Viola-da-Braccio

Treble (or Descant)

It is interesting to note how they were played and how the bow was held:

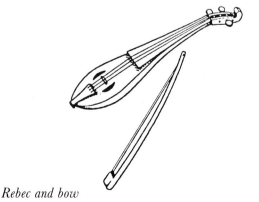

Rebec and bow

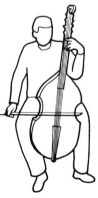

| *Treble* | *Tenor* | *Bass* |

Viol bow and hand position – compare the German method of holding the double bass bow (see page 29)

The tone of the viol is soft and delicate and by the beginning of the 18th century it was superseded by the more powerful and agile violin.

The finest violins at this time were made by three Italian instrument makers – Amati, Guarneri and Stradivari. Amazingly they all lived in the same town, Cremona, in Northern Italy.

The greatest of them all was Antonio Stradivari (*c.* 1644–1737). He produced over 1,000 instruments, 400 of which are thought to be in existence today. Though making mainly violins, he also made a few violas and cellos as well as other instruments such as bass viol and guitar.

The four strings of the violin are tuned in fifths:

The instrument is capable of playing most complicated music at great speed as well as lyrical passages of great beauty.

Johannes Brahms (1833–1897): *Symphony No. 3*

In the higher range the violin makes a brilliant sound, while in the lower register the sound is very resonant and strong, which is excellent for broad and expansive melodies. In the orchestra the violins are divided into two sections, called Violin I and Violin II. (This may be compared with the way Sopranos are divided up in a choir into firsts and seconds.)

NB Nearly everything mentioned about the violin on pages 24–25 applies to the viola, cello and double bass. These instruments basically differ in size, range and tonal quality of notes. The overall shape of each instrument is quite similar.

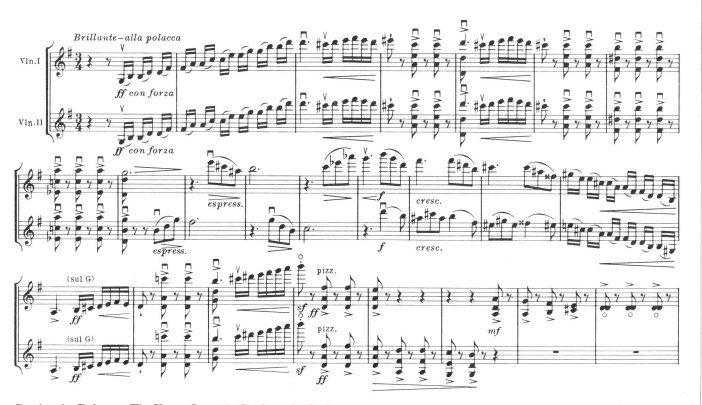

Benjamin Britten: *The Young Person's Guide to the Orchestra*

Viola

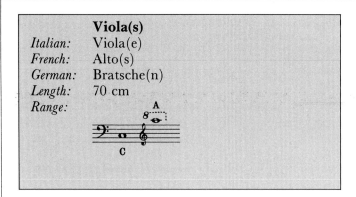

	Viola(s)
Italian:	Viola(e)
French:	Alto(s)
German:	Bratsche(n)
Length:	70 cm
Range:	

Viola and bow

This is the alto of the string family. As you will have noticed the French word for viola is *alto*. Like the violin it has four strings tuned in fifths:

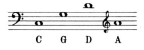

The normal clef for the viola is the alto (or C) clef:

If the music is high for a time and uses leger lines:

Dmitry Shostakovich: *Symphony No. 5*

then the music is written out in the treble (or G) clef:

The viola is larger and heavier than a violin and with its deeper notes it is generally less brilliant in sound, having a warmer, richer quality.

Comparative sizes of the stringed instruments

Cello

Violoncello(s)	
Italian:	Violoncello(i)
French:	Violoncelle(s)
German:	Violoncell(e)
Length:	130 cm
Range:	

Cello and bow

The cello (pronounced chello) is much too big to be played under the chin. So it is propped up on the floor by means of a spike pulled out from the bottom of the instrument. Originally players supported the instrument with their legs (compare the tenor viol on page 24).

The cello was developed in the 16th century and for nearly 150 years it existed alongside the very popular bass viol (viola-da-gamba).

It was at the beginning of the eighteenth century that the bass viol gave way to the cello in the same way that the treble viol gave way to the violin.

The four strings of the cello are tuned in fifths and are exactly one octave lower than the viola:

The cello has a rich penetrating sound and often plays soaring melodies as well as providing a bass line for the other strings. It has the widest dynamic range of all the strings.

Pyotr Tchaikovsky: *Symphony No. 6*

Music for the cello is mainly written in the bass (or F) clef. For high notes the tenor (or C)* clef is used:

and even the treble (or G) clef for very high notes.

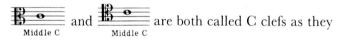 are both called C clefs as they 'fix' the position of middle C.

The C clef is movable.

String section playing pizzicato

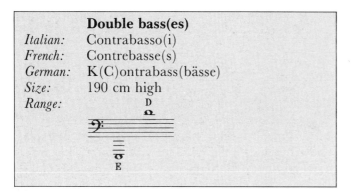

	Double bass(es)
Italian:	Contrabasso(i)
French:	Contrebasse(s)
German:	K(C)ontrabass(bässe)
Size:	190 cm high
Range:	

The double bass, the largest and deepest member of the violin family was developed in the 16th century from the violone, the double bass viol.

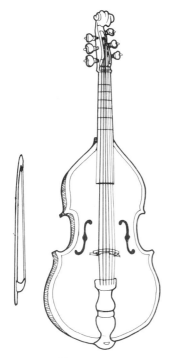

Double bass viol and bow

Two characteristics of the viols are found in the design of the double bass:
1 The shoulders slope more, and
2 The back of the instrument is flatter.
This enables the player, who either has to stand or sit on a high stool, to reach around the instrument and in particular to be able to play the notes at the end of the fingerboard, near the bridge.

Towards the end of the 18th century the double bass had three strings generally tuned to:

The double bass is a transposing instrument and all written notes sound an octave lower:

The need to write an octave higher than the actual sounds is clearly necessary to avoid leger lines below the stave.

It was for the three-stringed bass that Beethoven wrote. This was the standard double bass until early in the nineteenth century when four strings became the norm which has remained up to the present day:

Some double basses today have five strings, with the extra string going down to the C, a major third below the low E:

The strings of the double bass are so long and thick that ordinary pegs used on the other string instruments are not strong enough. Machine heads are used:

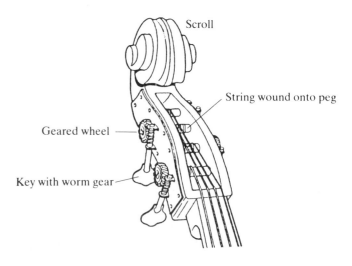

Double bass machine heads

The bow can be held in one of two ways:

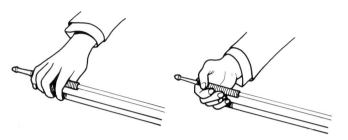

The French method *The German method*

(Compare this with holding the viol bow – page 25)

In the picture opposite the two players at the first desk of double basses are using these two methods.

The chief function of the double bass, often called bass, is to provide a strong harmonic foundation. Most of the time is spent in playing in octaves with the cellos. However, variety is frequently achieved by playing pizzicato which lightens the bass line and general orchestral texture.

The instrument is very capable of playing melodies:

Note the double bass bowing holds

Camile Saint-Saëns (1835–1921): *The Elephant* from *Carnival of the Animals*

Composers have now written music that demands great agility in bowing and fingering with wide leaps and complicated rhythms:

Richard Strauss (1864–1949): *Ein Heldenleben*

Harp

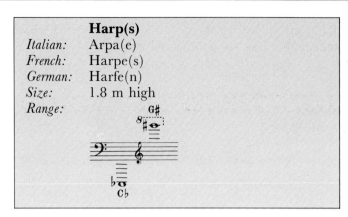

	Harp(s)
Italian:	Arpa(e)
French:	Harpe(s)
German:	Harfe(n)
Size:	1.8 m high
Range:	

The harp is one of the oldest instruments and is said to have originated from the twanging of a bow as used by an archer.

In its early stages, the harp had few strings, but the modern instrument has 47 strings. Each string is graded in length – the higher the pitch, the shorter the strings. As there are so many strings, to help the player, all the C strings are coloured red and the F strings are blue.

The harp has seven pedals which are operated by the feet. Each pedal controls one note of the octave eg one pedal controls all the D strings, another the C strings and so on:

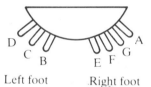

Left foot   Right foot

A concert harp

Each pedal can be placed into three positions which means that the string can produce three notes:

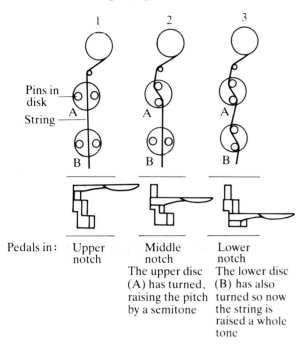

Each pedal is connected with the pins on the neck of the harp by wires running up inside the pillar:

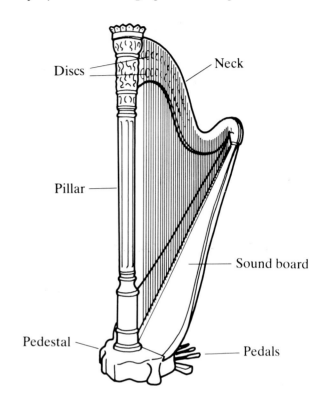

The harp strings are tuned to the scale of C♭ major:

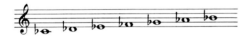

So taking the C♭ string as an example, when the pedal is in the upper notch (1), the string will sound C♭. This is called the 'flat' position. When the pedal is in the middle notch (2) the string rises a semitone, which is C natural. This is called the 'natural' position. When the pedal is in the lower position, the string rises a further semitone, and so the string will sound C♯. This is called the 'sharp' position.

The music for a harp is written on two staves like a piano. (The music for all the other orchestral instruments so far mentioned is written on one stave.)

The harpist can play single notes, a melody with an accompaniment and full chords with usually four notes to each hand as the little finger is not used.

One special effect characteristic of the harp is the glissando which is made by the player's hand (or hands) sweeping across the strings.

Benjamin Britten: *The Young Person's Guide to the Orchestra*

Percussion

Timpani or Kettledrums

Theme E for Percussion – Benjamin Britten: *The Young Person's Guide to the Orchestra*

Percussion instruments are struck and/or shaken, and are the most ancient of instruments. They are divided into two groups – those that give definite pitch (tuned) and those of indefinite pitch (untuned). One important point to remember about percussion instruments is that a tremendous variety of sound can be obtained according to the sticks or beaters used.

NB The details and history of percussion instruments are so complex and concern so many instruments that it is impossible to do justice to them here.
A recommended book on this fascinating subject is: *Percussion Instruments and their History*, by James Blades, published by Faber and Faber.

Compass of Tuned Percussion

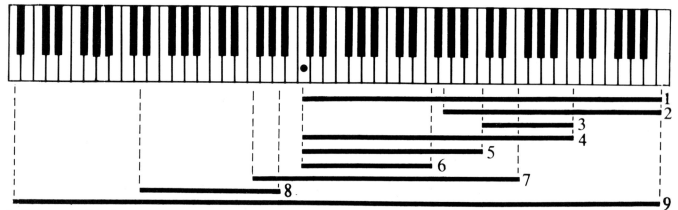

1 Celesta 2 Glockenspiel 3 Crotales 4 Xylophone 5 Keyboard Glockenspiel 6 Tubular bells 7 Vibraphone 8 Timpani 9 Pianoforte

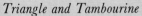

Triangle and Tambourine

Side Drum

Cymbals

Bass Drum

Instruments of definite pitch

Timpani or Kettledrums

Italian: Timpani
French: Timbales
German: Pauken

Range and
head diameters:

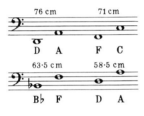

There are at least two timpani in the orchestra. Each instrument consists of a calf skin or plastic drum head stretched over a copper or a fibreglass bowl. The notes are tuned by tightening or slackening the skin by:

1   taps or handles around the rim:

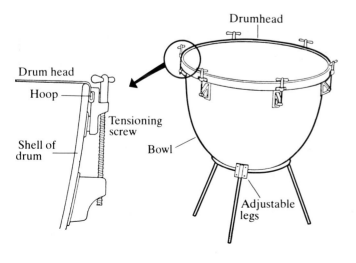

NB   In the 19th century some timpani were tuned by a single handle to reduce time needed for tuning:

2   a pedal which controls the tuning by using the foot:

At the top is a tuning gauge which shows the pitch:

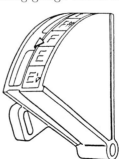

33

(Timpani continued)

Changes of pitch can now be made quickly by using pedals, which has meant that timpani can be used for playing tunes and for special effects such as glissandi.

Béla Bartók (1881–1945):
Music for Strings, Percussion and Celesta

In the orchestra it is usual for a player to be the timpani specialist. The other percussionists have to play the rest of the instruments specified in the score.

Glockenspiel

Italian: Campanelli
French: Carillon
German: Glockenspiel
Range:

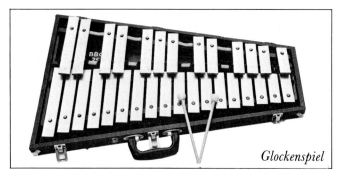

Glockenspiel

This German word means 'play of bells' which aptly describes the instrument. It consists of two rows of metal bars which give a bell-like sound. Various kinds of mallets are used.

Music for the glockenspiel sounds two octaves higher than written:

You can see why the music is written two octaves lower than it sounds as many leger lines can be confusing to read:

Xylophone

Italian: Xy(i)lofono
French: Xylophone
German: Xylophon
Range:

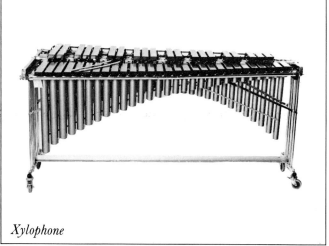

Xylophone

The word xylophone comes from the Greek *xylon* – wood and *phone* – voice. Below the bars are suspended tube resonators in which the air column frequency matches the pitches of the bars. This enriches the sound. The bars are usually made of rosewood.

Music for the xylophone is either written at its true pitch (in the treble clef) or if use would be made of leger lines, an octave lower than the actual sounds. Sometimes composers do not give clear instructions regarding pitch, so the player will select at which pitch to play.

Vibraphone

Italian: Vibrafono
French: Vibraphone
German: Vibraphon
Range:

The bars are made of steel. Like the xylophone, a resonating tube hangs beneath each bar. But at the top of each tube is a revolving disc, powered by electricity which alternately opens and closes the tube. This causes the note to 'wobble'.

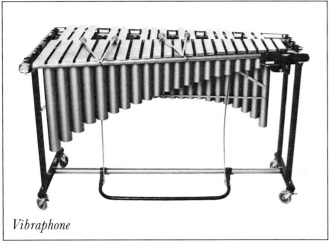

Vibraphone

The foot pedal is used to allow the notes to be sustained (compare this with the sustaining pedal on the piano). The vibraphone can be played without the use of the revolving discs and without electricity.

Music for the vibraphone is normally written at actual pitch.

Tubular Bells

Italian: Campane
French: Cloches
German: Glocken
Range:

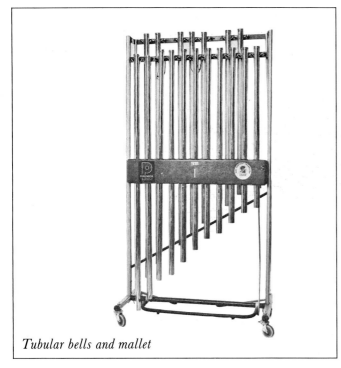

Tubular bells and mallet

The standard orchestral tubular bells consists of 18 steel tubes graded in length to give the different pitches.

The tubes are usually played near the top by a wooden mallet:

Music is written for Tubular Bells at actual pitch.

Crotales

Italian: Crotali (Cimbali antichi)
French: Crotales (Cymbales antiques)
German: Antiken Zimbeln
Range:

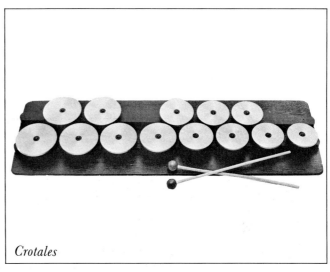

Crotales

Crotales (a French word) are really metal castanets, resembling small cymbals. These cymbals, also called Antique cymbals, were used by chiefly French composers in the 19th century who specified pitched notes. Hector Berlioz, for example, wrote for two pairs of these cymbals sounding:

in *Romeo and Juliet* (1839).

These instruments were made to his instructions. Soon other composers were writing for the crotales at different pitches with the result that nowadays they have been made into a chromatically-tuned set, played by a beater. Music is written an octave lower than the actual sounds.

Celesta

Italian: Celeste
French: Celesta
German: Celeste
Range:

The celesta, patented by Auguste Mustel in 1886 is really a keyboard glockenspiel. It has a series of small metal bars which are struck by small hammers, when piano-type keys are played. Beneath each metal bar is a box resonator. At the base of the instrument is a sustaining pedal. Music for the celesta is written on two staves (as the harp and piano) and is written an octave lower than the actual sounds.

NB   To the right of the player can be seen a Keyboard Glockenspiel. Like the celesta, it has a pianoforte-type action with a range of:

Music is generally written an octave lower than the actual sounds and is written on two staves. It was used by Wolfgang Mozart (1756–1791) in his opera *The Magic Flute* to represent the little bells of Papageno.

Pianoforte

Italian: Pianoforte
French: Piano
German: Klavier
Range:

Action of Upright Piano

A *Strings*   E *Dampers*
B *Wrest pins*   F *Frame*
C *Hammers*   G *Pedal levers*
D *Soundboard*   H *Pedals*

The pianoforte is included in the percussion section as a number of writers on the instruments of the orchestra place it in this section (the hammers strike the strings). However it can be argued that the pianoforte may also be included in the string family.

A Grand Piano

Side Drum

Italian: Tamburo
French: Tambour (Caisse claire)
German: Kleine Trommel
Size: 38 cm in diameter

This is a small drum, played by two wooden drumsticks. It has a skin at either end of a shallow cylinder. Three or four gut strings or wires called a snare, lie across the lower skin, which rattle on this skin when the drum is played. A small lever on the side releases the snare if this rattle effect is not required.

Tenor Drum

Italian: Tamburo rullante
French: Caisse roulante
German: Rührtrommel

The Tenor Drum is a deeper side drum without the snares.

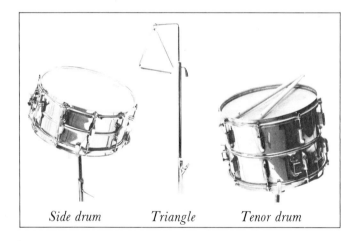

Side drum   Triangle   Tenor drum

Bass Drum

Italian: Gran cassa
French: Grosse caisse
German: Grosse trommel
Size: Diameter – up to 100 cm
  Width – up to 50 cm

This is the largest orchestral drum and is usually played with a large padded drumstick. The sound is very low and booming and though effective played quietly, it is often used with the full orchestra especially in a tremendous climax.

A Bass drum

Triangle

Italian: Triangolo
French: Triangle
German: Triangel

This is a metal instrument bent into a triangle with one corner open. This opening prevents a sound of definite pitch. Triangles can be of various sizes. It is played by being struck with a metal beater. Besides single beats, it can be used for a trill, with the beater being played quickly from side to side in the upper corner.

Tambourine

Italian: Tamburino
French: Tambour de Basque
German: Tamburin

This is a small hand drum with jingles in the frame. Tambourines can come in various sizes with an equally varying number of jingles. The instrument can be played by striking the head (or wooden rim) with the knuckles, fist, fingertips, back of the hand or on the player's knee. It can be shaken in the air (a jingle roll) or played with a moistened thumb, run across the skin so that it rebounds quickly causing the drumhead and jingles to sound. This is a thumb trill. The tambourine can also be played by beaters.

Cymbals

Suspended Cymbals

Italian:	Piatti (A due; A2)	Piatto sospeso
French:	Cymbales	Cymbale suspendue
German:	Becken	Becken (hangend)
Size:	Up to 66 cm in diameter	

Tam-Tam

Italian:	Tam-tam
French:	Tam-tam
German:	Tam-tam
Size:	up to 150 cm in diameter

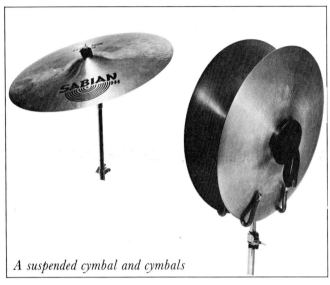

A suspended cymbal and cymbals

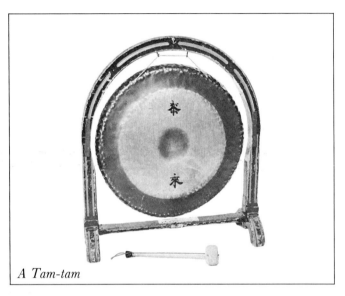

A Tam-tam

These are two plates of metal played by being clashed together. They are chiefly used to highlight an orchestral climax. A cymbal may be used singly by being suspended in the middle and played by a stick, a wire brush, or indeed a variety of beaters.

This is a large bronze disc of oriental origin with the rim turned down all around so that the edge does not vibrate. The beater usually has a soft head though other types of beaters have been requested for special effects. The Tam-Tam does not give a note of definite pitch, but a Gong may be tuned to a specific note.

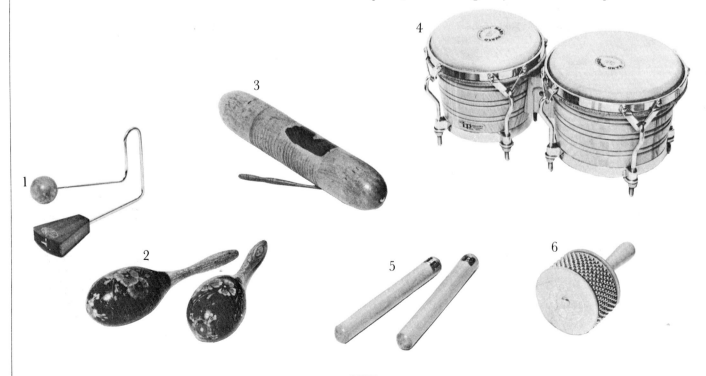

Other percussion instruments

		Italian	French	German
1	**Vibraslap**	Vibraslap	Vibraslap	Vibraslap
2	**Maracas**	Marache	Maracas (Boîte à clous)	Maracas
3	**Raspel**	Guiro	Rape Guero	Raspel
4	**Bongos**	Bongos	Bongos	Bongos
5	**Claves**	Claves	Claves	Claves
6	**Cabasa**	Cabasa	Cabasa	Cabasa
7	**Castanets**	Castagnette (Nacchere)	Castagnettes	Kastagnetten
8	**Woodblock**	Cassa di legno	Bloc de bois	Holztrommel Blocke
9	**Chinese block** (Temple block)	Ceppi Chinois	Blocs chinois	Chinesische Blocke
10	**Ratchet**	Raganella	Crécelle	Ratsche (Knarre)
11	**Sleighbells**	Sonagli	Grelots	Schellen
12	**Antique Cymbals** (See page 35)	Crotali	Crotales	Antiken Zimbeln
13	**Whip**	Frusta (Flagello)	Fouet	Holzklapper (Peitsche)
14	**Cowbells**	Cencerro	Sonnaille	Almeuglocke

The number of percussion instruments required by composers today are seemingly limitless, certainly far too many to be mentioned in this book. For example composers have written for: anvils, chains, sirens, car horns, whistles, birdcalls, lion's roar, thunder, breaking of glass, typewriter and ticking of clocks.

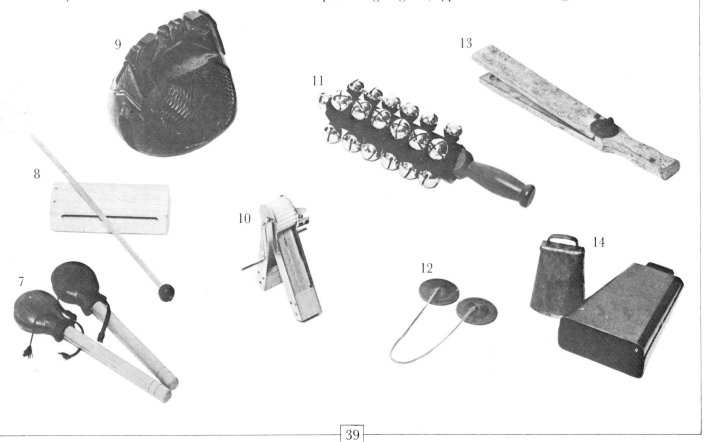

The word Orchestra comes from a Greek word meaning 'a dancing place'. This goes back to around the 5th century BC to when plays were performed in open air theatres (amphitheatres).

In front of the main acting area was a space for singers, dancers and instrumentalists. It was this space that was called Orchestra.

Nowadays, orchestra refers to a large group of musicians playing together, the exact number depending on the kind of music. This 'organised' group of instrumentalists really came into being at the start of the 18th century. Before this, the ensembles consisted of a varying, haphazard collection of players, often made up of musicians who were available in the locality. But by the 1700s it was generally agreed that the orchestra should consist of:

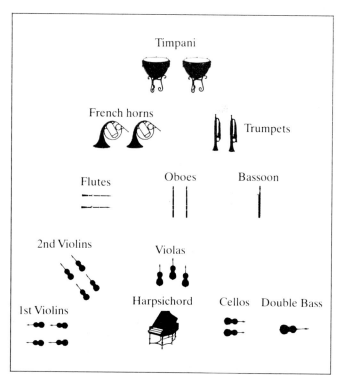

Even the line-up varied in numbers and combination of instruments. The harpsichord player and sometimes the first violinist directed the orchestra.

By 1800 the orchestra had grown to around:

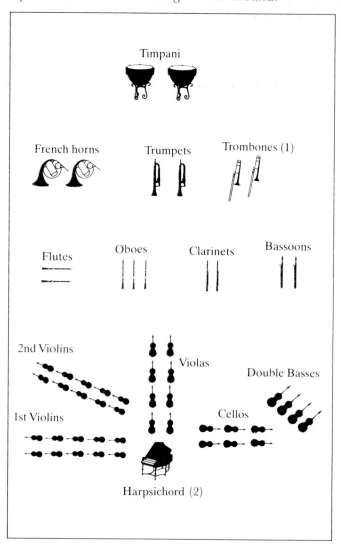

1   Trombones were mainly used in opera orchestras.
2   Many performances were still conducted from the harpsichord. Joseph Haydn (1732–1809) directed his late symphonies from the keyboard and Muzio Clementi (1752–1832) conducted from the keyboard in London in 1828.

the Orchestra

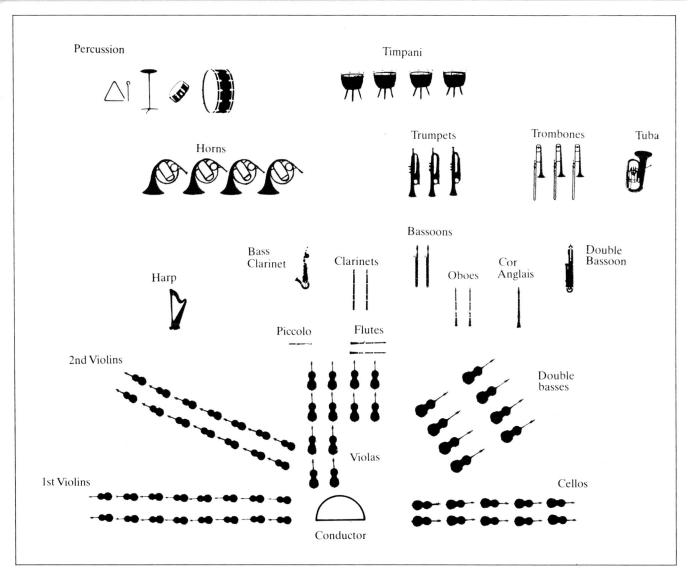

The nineteenth century saw an enormous expansion of the orchestra and by the middle of the century it had developed into the grouping above.

By the 20th century composers were writing for orchestras of immense size, including 6 timpani, 8 horns, 4 trumpets, 4 trombones, 2 tubas, 2 harps, extra woodwind, celesta, extra percussion and extra strings to balance up the overall sound.

During this century, the smaller orchestra (chamber orchestra) returned. Some are based on the 18th century type orchestra and are used by composers who want to get away from the huge, often Romantic-sounding orchestra. New ways of playing instruments have been explored. Electronic instruments have been introduced as well as pre-recorded tapes.

The Conductor

When an orchestra meets and rehearses a work, the conductor's job is to make sure that the players keep together, and that the various sections blend. The conductor has a responsible position as he has to interpret the composer's markings, which means such things as how loud or how soft the music has to be played, how much to make of crescendi (gradually getting louder) or diminuendi (gradually getting softer), to set the tempi and to make sure that the beginnings and endings of sections and movements are neat and together. The most important part of his work is done in rehearsals, when all these points are carefully worked at. Most conductors use a small stick called a baton, to give various indications, though many use in addition a nod, a raising of an eye-brow, a wink, as well as other body movements.

Sir Henry Wood (1869–1944) a famous English conductor mentioned the following points:

1   A conductor must have a complete general knowledge of music.

2   The conductor must have more than a slight acquaintance with every instrument of the orchestra, and if possible, some intensive study of a stringed instrument – preferably the violin.

3   The conductor must play the piano well.

4   The conductor must have an impeccably sensitive ear, as well as rhythmic and interpretative sense.

5   The conductor must be unafraid of the art of gesture.

6   The conductor must be a perfect sight-reader and sound musician.

7   The conductor must study the art of singing.

8   The conductor must have a good physique, a good temper, and a strong sense of discipline.

The author conducting

A Selection of Music for Listening

Here are some examples of music illustrating instruments. (Dates of a composer are given only with the first mention of that composer.)

Piccolo
Malcolm Arnold (b1921) *English Dance No. 5*
Georges Bizet (1838–1875) *Farandole (l'Arlésienne)*
John Philip Sousa (1854–1932) *March – The Stars and Stripes for ever*
Pyotr Tchaikovsky (1840–1893) *Chinese Dance (Nutcracker)*
Antonio Vivaldi (1678–1741) *Piccolo Concerti in C and A minor*

Flute
Johann Sebastian Bach (1685–1750) *Rondo and Badinerie (Suite in B minor)*
Luciano Berio (b1925) *Sequenza I* for solo flute
John Cage (b1912) *Solo (1958)* for flute, piccolo and alto flute
Claude Debussy (1862–1918) *Syrinx* for solo flute
Christoph Gluck (1714–1787) *Dance of the Blessed Spirits (Orfeo)*
Jacques Ibert (1890–1962) *Flute Concerto*
Wolfgang Amadeus Mozart (1756–1791) *Flute Concerti in G and D*
Carl Nielsen (1865–1931) *Flute Concerto*
Sergey Prokofiev (1891–1953) *Peter and the Wolf*
Edgard Varèse (1883–1965) *Density 21.5* for solo flute

Alto Flute
Maurice Ravel (1875–1937) *Daphnis et Chloé*
Igor Stravinsky (1882–1971) *The Rite of Spring*

Oboe
Ludwig van Beethoven (1770–1827) *Trio for 2 oboes and cor anglais*
Luciano Berio *Sequenza VII* for solo oboe
Georges Bizet *Symphony in C (2nd movement)*
Benjamin Britten (1913–1976) *Six Metamorphoses after Ovid* for solo oboe
George Frideric Handel (1685–1759) *Arrival of the Queen of Sheba (Solomon)* – 2 oboes
Bohuslav Martinů (1890–1959) *Oboe Concerto*
Sergey Prokofiev *Peter and the Wolf*
Franz Schubert (1797–1828) *Symphony No. 9 (2nd movement)*
Ralph Vaughan Williams (1872–1958) *Oboe Concerto*

Cor Anglais
Hector Berlioz (1803–1869) *Symphonie Fantastique (3rd movement)* – opening contrasts cor anglais with oboe
Arthur Bliss (1891–1975) *Sextet for Strings, Harp and Cor Anglais*
Aaron Copland (b1900) *Quiet City* for cor anglais, trumpet and strings
Antonín Dvořák (1841–1904) *Symphony No. 9 (2nd movement)*
César Franck (1822–1890) *Symphony in D minor (2nd movement)*
Jean Sibelius (1865–1957) *The Swan of Tuonela*

Oboe d'amore
Johann Sebastian Bach (arr Tovey) *Concerto in A*
Claude Debussy *Images (3rd movement)*
Richard Strauss (1864–1949) *Symphonia Domestica (Scherzo)*

Clarinet
Johannes Brahms (1833–1897) *Clarinet Quintet in B minor*
Aaron Copland *Clarinet Concerto*
Wolfgang Amadeus Mozart *Clarinet Concerto*
Wolfgang Amadeus Mozart *Symphony No. 39 (Trio of Minuet)*
Sergey Prokofiev *Peter and the Wolf*
Igor Stravinsky *Three pieces for clarinet solo*
Carl Maria Weber (1786–1826) *2 Clarinet Concerti (Op. 73 and 74)*

Bass Clarinet
Alois Hába (1893–1973) *Suite for Solo Bass Clarinet*
Pyotr Tchaikovsky *Dance of the Sugar Plum Fairy (Nutcracker)* – good illustration of Celesta

Saxophones
Georges Bizet *Prelude to l'Arlésienne* (alto)
Claude Debussy *Rhapsodie* (alto)
Alexander Glazunov (1865–1936) *Concerto for alto saxophone*
Alexander Glazunov *Quartet for saxophones* (soprano, alto, tenor and bass)
Jacques Ibert *Concertino da camera* (alto)
Modest Musorgsky (1839–1881) (orch Ravel) *The Old Castle* from *Pictures from an Exhibition* (alto)

Bassoon
Malcolm Arnold *English Dance No. 3*
Georges Bizet *Les Dragons D'Alcala – Prelude to Act 2 – (Carmen)*
Wolfgang Amadeus Mozart *Bassoon Concerto*
Sergey Prokofiev *Peter and the Wolf*
Igor Stravinsky *The Rite of Spring* (opening)
Carl Maria Weber *Bassoon Concerto*

Double Bassoon
Ernö Dohnányi (1877–1960) *Variations on a Nursery Song* – Variation 4 – in duet with piccolo
Maurice Ravel *Piano Concerto for Left Hand* – opening

Horn
Benjamin Britten *Serenade for Tenor, Horn and Strings*
Wolfgang Amadeus Mozart *Horn Concerti Nos. 1–4*
Sergey Prokofiev *Peter and the Wolf* – 3 horns
Nikolay Rimsky-Korsakov (1844–1908) *Notturno* – 4 horns
Robert Schumann (1810–1856) *Konzertstück* – 4 horns
Michael Tippett (b1905) *Sonata for 4 horns*

Trumpet
Johann Altenburg (1734–1801) *Concerto for 7 trumpets and timpani*
Johann Sebastian Bach *Brandenburg Concerto No. 2* – with flute and violin soli
Aaron Copland *Quiet City* for cor anglais, trumpet and strings
George Frideric Handel *Aria – The trumpet shall sound (Messiah)*
Joseph Haydn (1732–1809) *Trumpet Concerto*
Leoš Janáček (1854–1928) *Sinfonietta* – 12 trumpets
Modest Musorgsky (orch Ravel) *Samuel Goldenberg and Schmuyle (Pictures at an Exhibition)* – muted trumpet

Cornet
Sergey Prokofiev *Lieutenant Kijé*
Igor Stravinsky *Petrouchka*
Igor Stravinsky *Royal March (The Soldier's Tale)*

Trombone
Malcolm Arnold *Fantasy for Trombone* – unaccompanied
Luciano Berio *Sequenza V*
Vinko Globokar (b1934) *Discourse II* – with tape
Gordon Jacob (1895–1984) *Trombone Concerto*
Wolfgang Amadeus Mozart *Tuba Mirum (Requiem)*
Nikolay Rimsky-Korsakov *Trombone Concerto*

Tuba
George Kleinsinger (1914–1982) *Tubby the Tuba*
Ralph Vaughan Williams *Tuba Concerto*

Violin
Johann Sebastian Bach *6 solo sonatas (Partitas)*
Bêla Bartók (1881–1945) *Violin Concerto* and *Sonata for unaccompanied violin*
Ludwig van Beethoven *Violin Concerto* and *Two Romances*
Alban Berg (1885–1935) *Violin Concerto*
Johannes Brahms *Violin Concerto* and *Double Concerto* for violin and cello
Felix Mendelssohn (1809–1847) *Violin Concerto*
Wolfgang Amadeus Mozart *6 Violin Concerti* and *Sinfonia Concertante* for violin and viola
Niccolò Paganini (1782–1840) *24 Caprices* for unaccompanied violin
Jean Sibelius *Violin Concerto*
Johann Strauss (1844–1899) and Josef Strauss (1827–1870) *Pizzicato Polka*
Pyotr Tchaikovsky *Violin Concerto*
Anton Webern (1883–1945) *4 Pieces* (Op. 7)

Viola
Johann Sebastian Bach *Brandenberg Concerto No. 6*
Bêla Bartók *Viola Concerto*
Hector Berlioz *Harold in Italy*
Luciano Berio *Sequenza VI* for solo viola
Max Bruch (1838–1920) *Double Concerto* for clarinet and viola
Zoltán Kodály *Song (Háry János)*
Karlheinz Stockhausen (b1928) *Kurzwellen*
Georg Telemann (1681–1767) *Viola Concerto*
William Walton (1902–1983) *Viola Concerto*

Cello
Johann Sebastian Bach *6 unaccompanied suites*
Ernest Bloch (1880–1959) *Schelomo*
Johannes Brahms *Piano Concerto No. 2* (opening of 3rd movement)
Benjamin Britten *Cello Symphony*
Antonín Dvořák *Cello Concerto*
Edward Elgar (1857–1934) *Cello Concerto*
Camille Saint-Saëns (1835–1921) *2 Cello Concerti*
Franz Schubert *Symphony No. 8* (1st movement, 2nd theme
Dmitry Shostakovich (1906–1975) *2 Cello Concerti*
Pyotr Tchaikovsky *Variations on a Rococo Theme*
Iannis Xenakis (b1922) *Nomos alpha*